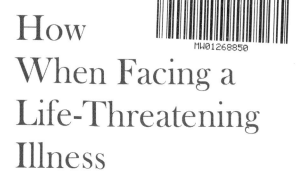

How
When Facing a
Life-Threatening
Illness

Powerful Bible Reflections and
Promises to Heal Sickness, Boost
Strength and Encourage Your Faith
in God

Gedaliah Shay

Patent and Trademark Office by Biblica,
Inc.®

Table of Contents

INTRODUCTION 1

CHAPTER 1..7

CHRIST OUR HOPE 7

CHAPTER 2 22

REPENTANCE................................... 22

CHAPTER 3 32

PRAYER OF THE RIGHTEOUS...... 32

CHAPTER 4 44

OUR ATTITUDE IN TRYING TIMES: SICKNESS 44

CHAPTER 5 62

AN ACT OF FAITH 62

CHAPTER 6 78

GOD'S PROMISES CONCERNING LIFE-THREATENING ILLNESSES 78

CHAPTER 7 91

BELIEVE AND RECEIVE 91

PRAYER FOR PERFECT HEALING..104

CONCLUSION 108

INTRODUCTION

"What God cannot do, doesn't exist"

A life-threatening illness is debilitating enough to disrupt every facet of one's life.

The feeling of depression and hopelessness is quite easy to befall individuals with ill-health. However, the Word of God says, *"with God all things are possible."* God is a God of healing and sufficient Grace. He wants us to be whole and in perfect health. God is not just after the Spiritual wholeness but also that of the mind, soul, and body. Sickness is under the domain of God. He didn't establish it, but He has dominion and authority over it.

In this book, you can anticipate healing. Whether momentarily or instantaneously, it will definitely happen. If God heals you gradually, that implies that the illness you are going through is for a purpose to glorify the name of God. It could be for a sermon or the improvement of your character (unknown to you). You might have met someone or people who have inspired you through their affliction, and this adds up to your testimony.

It is important to talk to God about your pains, afflictions, and discomfort. He has to know the exact thing you want. Open up to Him and request that He commands His healing into your life. If it is His will to have you be that way, pray for divine comfort, wisdom, and strength to deal with the illness. It might not be the perfect treatment for your ailment, but these prayers would comfort you at this trying time.

This book will guide you on how to pray for that perfect healing during this time of fear, depression, and doubt.

These prayers do not necessarily have to be for you. You can say these prayers on behalf of someone going through a life-threatening illness at the moment. Keep them in your thoughts and pray these prayers of healing for them.

PRAYER POINTS FOR HEALING

- Lord Jesus, I thank You for bringing hope to Mankind. I pray that you direct divine doctors and treatments that would heal this illness to me.

- Lord Jesus, restore good health unto me.

- Help me to rest peacefully under your sheltering wings

- Ignite hope in my heart, Lord, restore hope and belief to my hopelessness

- Transform my tears to smiles

- Give me the discernment and wisdom to decide which treatments and hospital to use.

- In this moment of pain and afflictions, help me not to give in to bitterness, anger, resentment and unforgiveness. I don't want to become captive to sin. Refresh me in Christ Jesus.

- I thank You, Lord, because You are forever in control of my life, from my first to my final breath. You will always be in control.

CHAPTER 1

CHRIST OUR HOPE

"But he was pierced for our transgressions, he was crushed for our iniquities; the punishment that brought us peace was on him, and by his wounds, we are healed". (Isaiah 53:5)

The miraculous healing testimony of this one-time patient I saw in a hospital I worked in makes this verse of the Bible keep ringing in my heart over and over again. It shows nothing but God's endless grace to the fallen race of man. I could feel every line of the helpless man's word as he was relating his experience to me. I just couldn't get it out of my mind as I walked along the lonely path that led to my apartment.

It was very early on a Monday morning when every member of the clinic would be serious with their obligations at the office. Then I got this visitor whom I later recognized as my one-time patient with a dreadful sickness. With all my 25 years of experience in this medical profession, I couldn't fathom why the medications, treatments, and surgeries never worked out positive in healing this man. Even though the medical results revealed this strange illness to be the dreaded Covid-19 virus, but it felt as though there was more to it.

Like every other impossible critical situation, I had to give up on the patient and I told him to find a way of living with it and was he discharged hopelessly and helplessly. But presently, he is right here sitting before me, telling the miraculous story of how he got his healing.

This man struggled to live with this life-threatening illness for months after he was discharged. He worked in pains, discomfort and fear every passing day till he found the path that processed his healing. You can imagine how great and out of the world this man felt he got his recovery.

As he was relating his experience to me, he referred to Isaiah 53. The whole verses in this chapter confess nothing but grace for an unworthy fallen race. Take a look at it.

"Who has believed our report? And to whom has the arm of the LORD been revealed?

53:2 For He shall grow up before Him as a tender plant, And as a root out of dry ground. He has no form or comeliness; And when we see Him, There is no beauty that we should desire Him.

53:3 He is despised and rejected by men, A Man of sorrows and acquainted with grief. And we hid, as it were, our faces from Him; He was despised, and we did not esteem Him.

53:4 Surely He has borne our griefs And carried our sorrows; Yet we esteemed Him stricken, Smitten by God, and afflicted.

53:5 But He was wounded for our transgressions, He was bruised for our iniquities; The chastisement for our peace was upon Him, And by His stripes, we are healed.

53:6 All we like sheep have gone astray; We have turned, everyone, to his own way; And the LORD has laid on Him the iniquity of us all.

53:7 He was oppressed and He was afflicted, Yet He opened not His mouth; He was led as a lamb to the slaughter, And as a sheep, before its shearers is silent, So He opened not His mouth.

53:8 He was taken from prison and from judgment, And who will declare His generation? For He was cut off from the land of the living; For the transgressions of My people He was stricken.

53:9 And they made His grave with the wicked - But with the rich at His death, Because He had done no violence, Nor was any deceit in His mouth.

53:10 Yet it pleased the LORD to bruise Him; He has put Him to grief. When You make His soul an offering for sin, He shall see His seed, He shall prolong His days, And the pleasure of the LORD shall prosper in His hand.

53:11 He shall see the labor of His soul, and be satisfied. By His knowledge, My righteous Servant shall justify many, For He shall bear their iniquities. (Isaiah 53:1-11 NKJV)

The above presents a picture of someone who deliberately made his life a sacrifice for some unworthy people. As this man took me down the memory lane of his health experience, he mentioned that he got his healing when he realized how much hope he has in Christ.

Many times, we go through unnecessary pains and bury our heads in worry unnecessarily. Knowing how much benefits you have in something or someone will give you the knowledge of how you can maximally use such a thing. This man had to go through months of pain that he could have avoided within 4 days because he believed he had to find a means to get himself healed. Not until he came across a friend who shed more light on the scripture did he realize all the pains and sacrifices needed for his healing had been completed by someone he barely knew.

Knowing God and the power of His grace, which is so rich, full, and free, gives us the ability to access Him any time, any day for our needs. It sounds too good to be true. But that's just what it is. Isaiah 53 states the weight of our HOPE. It explicitly explained what the sacrificial lamb had to pass through so he could repurchase us what we lost at the beginning of the world in the garden of Eden. Pains and illnesses are never to be managed, you have the one who knows and understands your every struggle. Build your trust in Him, believe Him, and cast your cares and burdens on Him.

"Casting your hope on Him, for He cares for you..." There is no type of healing you will seek in Christ that you will not get. Suppose my one-time patient with the deadly Covid-19 virus could receive his healing by realizing his ability in Christ and placing his hope in the free provision made for his recovery. In that case, I do not know what that sickness is that Jesus Christ has not been wounded for.

"And by His wounds, we are healed".

Prayers

Christ has paid all you needed to pay for your healing, even when you barely knew Him and never deserved it. Yet, He'd give you everything He's made free so that you might get healed.

Let us pray:

- Lift your voice in thanksgiving to God for His full grace, which has been made free for your healing.

- Ask for His forgiveness for neglecting His rich grace upon you

- Now pray that He cleanse you with His blood and make you qualified to enjoy all the provisions He has made for your healing

- You need to tell Him to give you the grace to put your hope in Him firmly. To rely on Him for your healing and not on your strength.

- Now, begin to pray for your healing using this particular verse in Isaiah 53:5 "But he was pierced for our transgressions, he was crushed for our iniquities; the punishment that brought us peace was on him, and by his wounds, we are healed".

- Make sure you strongly believe in these words because they are powerful and give life to every soul that believes in them. As you pray, also make use of the selected powerful bible verses below that tell more about your hope of healing in Christ:

- So do not fear, for I am with you; do not be dismayed, for I am your God. I will strengthen you and help you; I will uphold you with my righteous right hand. (Isaiah 41:10 NIV)

- But I will restore you to health and heal your wounds,' declares the Lord, 'because you are called an outcast, Zion for whom no one cares. (Jeremiah 30:17)

- Have mercy on me, Lord, for I am faint; heal me, Lord, for my bones are in agony. (Psalm 6:2)

- Lord my God, I called to you for help, and you healed me Psalm 30:2. (Make sure you use this emphatically with your strong faith, believing you've gotten your healing even if you can still feel the pain)

- No temptation has overtaken you, except what is common to mankind. And God is faithful; he will not let you be tempted

beyond what you can bear. But
when you are tempted, he will
also provide a way out so that
you can endure it.
(1Corinthians 10:13)

Just as I've said earlier, these are
powerful bible verses for you to use.
They assure you that your hope in
Christ is secured, and you can get
your healing at any time you need it.

CHAPTER 2

REPENTANCE

This chapter is one of self-searching and self-examination. You will take an intense check on your life to see if there is any iniquity in you.

Don't forget, the essence of this devotional is to get you healed from this sickness draining strength from you. But what is the use of claiming the powerful words and verses from the scripture, if there is sin in your heart? Sin only performs the duty of standing as an obstruction in getting your prayers answered. It would stand against you from totally gaining access to the full and free healing provision that has been made available for you in Christ. There is nothing as deadly as sin. There is nothing as bad as not being able to partake in God's blessings.

Therefore, before giving you a list of powerful points in the scriptures to pray with, I would want you to check yourself first. The Bible says, "If we say that we have no sin, we deceive ourselves, and the truth is not in us. If we confess our sins, He is faithful and just to forgive us our sins and to cleanse us from all unrighteousness." (1 john1:8-9). This verse of the bible has shown us that there is no such thing as a perfect person. Any human born of a woman cannot claim to be a saint from birth. The first work of grace has to be done in your life first so you can enjoy the provision of divine healing from God.

The process of repentance is very simple but important. You have to undergo this process to obtain divine healing from God. God may not always send His judgment when we err, but it is never expected that you stay back in your sins till judgment comes. The wise thing to do at the slightest sinful mistake is to ask for grace and forgiveness from God. In the Bible, the Children of Israel faulted and committed a grievous offense against God on their way back from Egypt. God didn't spare them because they were His chosen nation. He sent a serpent to sting them to death. Not until Moses cried unto God for mercy did they get a solution to their sickness.

Don't forget; it is the child the Father loves He corrects. God would not slack in reproving you, especially when He sees that you are going off the track and there is danger ahead. He could have tried devising means of getting your attention and focus back on Him, and it turns out futile. In situations like this, God could use sickness to lay hold on you. But until you repent of your sins and ask for the intervention of the cleansing blood, you will continue to agonize in pain. And in this case, no amount of encouraging words can heal you. All you need is mercy!

Moses made the image of a brazen serpent and hung it on a tree for everyone stung by the serpent; they experienced healing as they looked up to it. Imagine what would have happened to individuals who refuse to look to the brazen serpent after being bitten. This signifies the role of obedience and the magnitude of grace and mercy that can be enjoyed in repentance.

For the children of Israel, it was looking unto a serpent's statute hanged on a tree that would heal them from the snake bite. For you and me today, grace, mercy, joy, healing, peace, and redemption is designed to come from looking unto Christ, who was once hanged on the tree for our sins.

Also, there are other instances mentioned in the bible where people sinned against God, and He sent His judgment to them. Not until they cried for mercy were they healed. Numbers 12:1-13 indicates Miriam's leprosy due to her murmur against Moses, the anointed man of God. She became a leper and was hidden in a place until the seventh day when God healed her. I am sure she didn't just stay back there in isolation without pleading for mercy.

At times, God would deliberately allow some illnesses to come your way to make you see what he wants to show you. It could be a wrong deed you have done in the past that He wants you to correct; it could be that God wants to show you another dimension of His power or that He wants to see what you will do in some particular situations.

Job is a perfect Biblical example. But most times, sicknesses are a result of some of our inactions, and once you repent of these shortcomings and are forgiven, you are licensed to enjoy an abundance of divine healing.

Below are some selected powerful scriptures from the Word of God recommended for you to pray along with as you plead for mercy from God and repent of your sins

- Jeremiah 17:14 NKJV

"Heal me, O Lord, and I shall be healed; Save me, and I shall be saved, For You are my praise."

Pray for divine healing from God.

- Exodus 15:26 NKJV

"He said, *"If you diligently heed the voice of the Lord your God and do what is right in His sight, give ear to His commandments and keep all His statutes, I will put none of the diseases on you which I have brought on the Egyptians. For I am the Lord who heals you."* cling to these words and pray for divine strength to diligently heed the voice of the Lord.

- 2 Chronicles 7:14 NKJV

"if My people who are called by My name will humble themselves, and pray and seek My face, and turn from their wicked ways, then I will hear from heaven, and will forgive their sin and heal their land."

God has promised to heal your land. Do not relent in prayers, pray for the

spirit and the grace to humble
yourself.

- Jeremiah 33:6 NKJV

"Behold, I will bring it health and healing; I will heal them and reveal to them the abundance of peace and truth." The word of God gave this assurance, are you still doubting? Activate your belief. Don't stop yet. Persevere!

CHAPTER 3

PRAYER OF THE RIGHTEOUS

 We are living in a world with its noisome pestilence and heart-breaking news of all kind. Sadly enough, there is no respective description among its distribution across the face of the earth; the young fall sick just like the old do; the righteous and the unrighteous too. However, it is comforting to know that in the world of Christendom, we are not alone! We have fellow followers of Christ who are on this same track with us to cheer us when the need calls and to share our burdens with us in times of tribulation.

Before Jesus ascended to heaven, he didn't fail to make known to His disciples that there would be afflictions. As long as we are still in this human temple, otherwise called flesh, we would deal with sicknesses, diseases, and even death, but we are assured that Christ has overcome the world. Having known this fact, when a Christian falls sick, there is a guideline to follow:

"Is anyone among you suffering? Let him pray. Is anyone cheerful? Let him sing psalms.

Is anyone among you sick? Let him call for the elders of the church, and let them pray over him, anointing him with oil in the name of the Lord.

And the prayer of faith will save the sick, and the Lord will raise him up. And if he has committed sins, he will be forgiven.

Confess your trespasses to one another, and pray for one another, that you may be healed. The effective, fervent prayer of a righteous man avails much."

James 5:13-16 NKJV

In times of sickness, as Christians, you have to understand that you are not saved to walk the spiritual journey alone. There is no such thing as an isolated spiritual journey. We are pilgrims together with each other.

When life-threatening sicknesses appear, you can pray for yourself, but a significant step a Christian should take as recommended by the Holy Bible is to send for the church's elders. These Elders have been ordained to carry out this responsibility, and they will come and talk to you about your situation. You might be asked if you are conscious of any sins that you want to confess. If there be any, you are at freedom to confess to them as they will guide you through tracing your steps back to God. The Elders have also been authorized to anoint you

with oil as this symbolizes the Holy
Spirit, who is mighty to heal. They
will pray with you and for you with
the understanding and belief that
God can and does heal. But, you must
submit to His sovereign will, which
you can always trust. If He chooses to
heal you, give Him the glory because
it wasn't the oil nor the prayers that
healed you. It was God!

WHY DO WE HAVE TO CALL ON THE ELDERS?

It has been mentioned that God
has a plan for everything in our lives,
and he won't do anything outside
what He has said or written. In every
organization, there is a leadership

setting trained and trusted with their members' welfare, and as such, they are accountable to a higher authority. The elders are the ones who hold responsibility for us. Pastors, Ministers, Deacons/Deaconesses, etc., are all elders, and we should not hesitate to send for them whenever we fall sick.

Furthermore, their collective prayers serve as intercession for us before God who will always honor such intercessory prayers. We might have the grace of receiving answers to our prayers whenever we pray alone, but we still have to send for the elders at times like this. It is not a matter of decision, it is God's instruction, and each of His instructions are to be obeyed. *"And Samuel said, Hath the LORD as great delight in burnt offerings and sacrifices, as in obeying the voice of the LORD? Behold, to obey is better than sacrifice, and to hearken than the fat of rams"* [1Samuel 15:22]. From this verse, we can see that our obedience provokes response first before our faith. God honors men who pay attention to instructions.

Another point we can take to knowledge in the prayers of the elders is that their prayer can stand in for us when our faith is weak or feeble. That is why the Bible says the prayer of faithful (that which is coming from righteous men of God) will heal the sick; even if the fellow may have sinned unknowingly, the intercession of the righteous stand in to occupy the broken bridge. *"The effectual fervent prayer of the righteous avail much"*.

The first example before us is the story of Miriam among her brothers, Aaron and Moses. Miriam was the first female prophet in Israel, and she had been a person who discharged her duties accordingly. Still, at a point in her life, she sinned against God and suffered leprosy for seven days. During her seven days behind the camp of the righteous, the children of God, more especially, Moses and Aaron, spent days before the Lord interceding for her at that time when she was unfit to pray for herself because of her sin. Eventually, God honored the prayer of the righteous and healed her. Here we can see why the blessing of the righteous is important. It doesn't connote that God cannot heal us when we pray for ourselves in times of illness, but this is God's plan, and it should be adhered strictly to.

Whatever ordeals you are going through, "Pray!" It is easy to sit on a spot and nod in agreement, but the question is, "When you experience complications, sicknesses, and hardships, is prayer your first response?" It is certainly not a natural reaction. If left to the flesh, the natural response to sicknesses and suffering is to moan, weep, complain, or throw a pity party. Or, we question God: "Why is this happening to me?" But James counters all this with the single word: "Pray!"

PRAYER POINTS

Having seen the light of the matter, you must respond to God through prayer; below are a few points that you should add to your prayer.

- Firstly, appreciate the Father for the exposition of this message. Thank Him for His good intentions to make you grow in His all-dimensional Grace.

- Ask Him to come into your
  heart if you haven't made him
  your personal Lord and Savior,
  and if you have, then you may
  rededicate your life to him.

- Request for grace to always
  abide by what God says in his
  word. God exalts his words
  more than he regards his
  name. Obeying what he says is
  of more importance than what
  sacrifice we have to offer to
  him.

- Ask Him to help you grow in
  His knowledge and grace
  according to the measure of
  Christ.

- Appreciate him for the answered prayer.

CHAPTER 4

OUR ATTITUDE IN TRYING TIMES: SICKNESS

Have you ever been so sick? Or do you have a relative who is so down with a life-threatening illness? I have been in that shoe several times, but God wants to let us know how to act in such times. I know how challenging, frustrating, and demanding these times can be, but our Father, who understands us, has prepared what we can do in times like this. The attitude you exhibit towards that ailment could determine if you would get your healing or not.

Trials have been in existence since sin got into the world. The Bible also has a lot of examples provided in the scriptures to help us know how to guide our attitude in trying. As we have known in the first chapter of this book that Christ is our only hope in seasons of distress and failing health. We also want to know how to act in trying times. Periods that do not seem palatable to us as the case may be.

In trying times, we are faced with options as to whether we should pray for healing, strength, or thank God. I want us to know that some sicknesses are to draw us back to God when we have left Him. Some are even to test our stand as Christians, and Job is an example we would look into.

I want you to know that the devil knows about your faithfulness to God. In Job 1 & 2, we see a wealthy man lose all his wealth, family, and even health because God wanted to confirm His stance to him or the devil. Reading through a few verses from the book of Job; we can see that Job only wanted to know why everything befell him, and he made his innocence known to God. The Bible records that Job did not sin against God nor curse God in all his trying times, even when his wife asked him to do so. Job also had three friends who discouraged him with the words of their mouth. Some things that happen to us are for reasons best known to God.

We would draw out practical steps from Job's case. We should note that;

1.   God knows all about us, and we should understand that His decision is final

2.   We should know that God cares about us and that His thoughts towards us are good, so when sicknesses seem to threaten us, our faith rests in those words of consolation.

3.   We should learn to be humble and let God speak rather than

declare our innocence,
questioning his judgment.

4.   When God is testing us, it is
      personal, and we might feel left
      alone, but rather than wasting
      time in misery, we should
      choose to fill our hearts with
      the voice, thoughts, and
      goodness of God.

Trying times are to bring out the
best in us because faith, hope,
strength, patience, and a host of
other beautiful qualities are
developed. God also draws us close to
him in trying times to let us shed
weights (weights may not necessarily
be sins, but devices that would make

our journey to becoming like Christ slower).

In trying times, I want you to know that healing is not the only thing to ask for, although this is very important. Let us quickly look at what the Bible says concerning our attitude in trying times;

1.   We can pray for healing:

In James 5:14 which says

14 Is any sick among you? let him call for the elders of the church; and let them pray over him, anointing him with oil in the name of the Lord:

15 And the prayer of faith shall save the sick, and the Lord shall raise him up; and if he have committed sins, they shall be forgiven him.

God can choose to heal us or not, but here is God giving us a simple logic. The prayer of faith in God shall save the sick!

But sometimes God chooses not to heal us, and at that points, He is calling our attention to something other than healing.

Let's have a look at the story of Lazarus in John 11. We would read through some selected verses

1.   *Now a certain man was sick, named Lazarus, of Bethany, the town of Mary and her sister Martha.*

4.   When Jesus heard that, he said, This sickness is not unto death, but for the glory of God, that the Son of God might be glorified thereby.

5.   When he had heard therefore that he was sick, he abode two days still in the same place where he was.

41. Then they took away the stone from the place where the dead was laid. And Jesus lifted up his eyes, and said, Father, I thank thee that thou hast heard me.

42.. I knew that thou hearest me always: but because of the people which stand by I said it , that they may believe that thou hast sent me.

43. And when he thus had spoken, he cried with a loud voice, Lazarus, come forth. [44] And he that was dead came forth, bound hand and foot with graveclothes: and his face was bound about with a napkin. Jesus saith unto them, Loose him, and let him go.

This is Jesus expressing His will. He could have quickly healed the sick, but he had a bigger plan to raise the dead!

Another thing to pray for when we are sick is to have God's peace.

2.   We can ask for peace:

Even in tough and trying times, your attitude should be that of hope. Be hopeful for good divine peace. God can still give you peace that passes human comprehension. Let us quickly see this in Philippians 4:7

"And the peace of God, which passeth all understanding, shall keep your hearts and minds through Christ Jesus."

Since God knows all, His will for us at such times might be to bestow us with peace even when we are hurting, and the pain might be excruciating, God's peace would be of comfort to us. In John 14:27 also, Christ assures us of his reassuring peace.

John 14:27

Peace I leave with you, my peace I give unto you: not as the world giveth, give I unto you. Let not your heart be troubled, neither let it be afraid.

The mind is the seat where every action stems from, so asking for divine peace would calm storms of doubts.

3.   We can also ask for strength

Strength is important in trying times because when all seem to fail, our strength as individuals can sustain us, but Christ remains the source of real power. Philippians 4:13 says

"I can do all things through Christ, which strengtheneth me."

Depending on your attitude in trying times, you can rejoice in dire times when your strength lies in God. You can smile when you have a loved one going through pain because of the strength you derive from Christ, and then you can hang on to God through His words to Paul in 2 Corinthians 12:9

And he said unto me, My grace is sufficient for thee: for my strength is made perfect in weakness. Most gladly therefore will I rather glory in my infirmities, that the power of Christ may rest upon me.

4.   We can ask for wisdom

When wisdom is mentioned, I want you to know that you can ask God to give the medical personnel the right treatment to give to you. God has all the wisdom in the world, and since He is our Father, you should go to Him to ask Him and let Him know about this too.

James 1:5 says "If any of you lack wisdom, let him ask of God, that giveth to all men liberally, and upbraideth not; and it shall be given him."

Our Father wants to answer our unselfish requests!

He made science, and therefore is the Ultimate Scientist, Doctor and Healer!

We would go through a prayer list together soon after this last but important point.

5.   We should always go to God for purification

God wants you to maintain a healthy relationship with Him, even in trying times. But because we are human, we have our weaknesses, and we fail at times. We might have hurt God in a way, or we might have been unable to forgive those that hurt us. These little things might be a barrier to all our prayer requests. David realized this in Psalm 66:18 when he said "If I regard iniquity in my heart, the Lord will not hear me"

Seek to purify yourself always. Make conscious efforts to follow peace with all men because some illnesses may result from your trespasses towards God or man. Rather than lamenting that sickness or ailment, wear a positive attitude towards your healing and soak yourself for purification in the blood of Jesus.

Jesus tells us of this in Luke 11:4 "Luke 11:4 KJV

And forgive us our sins; for we also forgive every one that is indebted to us. And lead us not into temptation; but deliver us from evil."

I want you to know that God is loving, and He would accept you even with your scars when you return to Him. This is confirmed in 1 John 1:9 *"If we confess our sins, he is faithful and just to forgive us our sins, and to cleanse us from all unrighteousness."*

Finally, I want you to know that tough times do not last, but tough people do. Weeping may also endure for a night, but joy comes in the morning.

It is time to say some words of prayer sincerely. God honors sincere requests.

PRAYER POINTS

Connect with God in prayers through the prayer list below:

•Pray for healing and quick recovery from your illness.

•Pray for swift relief from pain and divine strength through the various procedures.

•Pray for divine faithfulness in the face of trials.

•Pray for the endurance to persevere in the place of prayers and face each day.

•Pray for the assistance you get from family, friends, and the Christian community.

•Pray that God would send you the best medical care and scientific expertise in aiding your healing.

•Pray for divine wisdom to make the best decisions towards your recovery.

Feel free to talk to God, your creator, about your health. He wants to hear you express yourself.

CHAPTER 5
AN ACT OF FAITH

Your healing will never be complete until you take specific actions yourself. No matter how powerful the words you speak in your life!

This fact became clear to me when I was sick. This illness would not let me eat as I choose or go about my normal activities; I was confined to my sick bed alone. At a time, I got exhausted of my sick life. I couldn't bear seeing the once healthy and energetic me looking so weak and wobbly, most especially when I have many duties to attend to.

Do you know what I did? I got up from my sickbed and started doing those things I needed to do. Truth be told, it wasn't easy, and it appeared out of common sense. Everybody would feel the right thing to do when you're sick is to stay confined to the sickbed and wait on people to take care of you. But for you to get your healing out of this threatening sickness, you need to act against typical human belief.

I started with that food I couldn't eat whenever I was sick. I started taking that meal. Then from there, I tried exhibiting some of my duties. I began to attend to my work one after the other. And I would have almost forgotten that I was sick by the time I finished those tasks. You would have to break boundaries and go beyond the normal if you want to get extraordinary healing for this life-threatening sickness.

Your common sense may get you common things, but most times, you have to go the extra mile to get the extraordinary. You will need to go beyond typical human belief to get your healing.

2 kings 5:1-15 tells us about Naaman, who was a man like every other man. He expected something unique from prophet Elisha for him

to get his healing. And so he thought it was abnormal for him to bathe in River Jordan. But that was the action of faith he needed to do to get his healing. That was his own "extra" step. Imagine Naaman going back to his house still a leper, all because he couldn't bathe seven times in the Jordan River.

You remember King Hezekiah too? "In those days Hezekiah was sick and near death. And Isaiah the prophet, the son of Amoz, went to him and said to him, *"Thus says the Lord: 'Set your house in order, for you shall die, and not live"*. Even after he got the news from the Prophet of God that he would die in his sickness, it was expected of any human to start putting his house in order, including his kingdom. But NO, King Hezekiah would love to have more days and years on earth, he made known his desire to God with tears, and YES, he got his wish. God sent a message of life to him through the same prophet that told him about his death. His prayers and act of faith earned him 15 more years to live. (2 Kings 20:1-5)

There are many other characters in the bible that got their healings because they took up actions that were beyond the ordinary.

There are many times in the bible when Jesus would command the sick to stand up and walk, carry their sickbeds, walk, or take up some other actions before getting their healing. The command may look out of the normal for human comprehension, but those are actions of faith, the extra step required for those sick people to get their healing.

St. Luke 8:43-48. The woman with the issue of blood did not mind going in between the large crowd that throng after Jesus. Even in her sick state, she managed and struggled to touch the hem of Jesus's garment, with faith in her heart that she would obtain her healing from there. And yes, she got the healing she craved.

For the man at the pool of Bethesda, it was just to answer a simple question asked by Jesus Christ. *"Will thou be made whole?"* St. John 5:1-15. And with that, he was commanded to take his sickbed and walk. And he did! He got healed from his 38 years old sickness.

There are times when it would appear as though all things you trusted for healing has failed you, and you may be discouraged in your journey to getting healed. But one thing will never fail you. And that is what this spirit-filled, seven chapters' devotional on your healing is about.

Do you remember what was said about faith in the bible? *"So Jesus said to them, "Because of your unbelief; for assuredly, I say to you, if you have faith as a mustard seed, you will say to this mountain, 'Move from here to there,' and it will move; and nothing will be impossible for you."* St. Matthew 17:20.

Some acts and words of faith are a necessary environment for healing to occur. When Jesus ministered in his hometown of Nazareth, the Scripture says, *"He could not do any miracles there ... and he was amazed at their lack of faith" (Mark 6:5-6).* Jesus naturally did not go out looking for sick people; they came to him for healing -- their coming was a sign of faith, or at least of curiosity. And when they arrive, Jesus occasionally asks a question to discern their faith or to encourage their faith. In two instances, blind men called out to Jesus. He asked them:

"Do you believe that I can do this?" (Matthew 9:28)

"What do you want me to do for you?" (Matthew 20:32)

This is not just a test, but an encouragement to faith, a stimulus to believe.

Jairus came asking Jesus to heal his daughter, but when messengers came from home to report her death, Jesus noticed Jairus faltering. *"Don't be afraid; just believe,"* Jesus assures him, *"and she will be healed" (Luke 8:50)*.

To the epileptic boy's father who asked if Jesus could do anything, Jesus replied, *"If you can believe. Everything is possible for him who believes."* Immediately the boy's father exclaimed, *"I do believe; help me overcome my unbelief!" (Mark 9:23)* But it wasn't only the father's faith involved in healing.

Too often, those with healing gifts blame lack of healing on the sick person rather than take responsibility for our lack of faith. Yes, "according to your faith will it be done to you" is a principle (as in Matthew 9:29), but it was Jesus' act of faith that accomplished the healing.

Commanding a mountain could be your extra step and action of faith in getting healed. It could be taking a walk once in a while rather than just sleeping on the sickbed. It could be a deliberate act of singing praises to God that will give you the miraculous victory over this life-threatening illness.

Whatever it is, you need to take obvious actions coupled with your faith and believe that you will get your healing. There is nothing faith in God cannot achieve. It may look so impossible for you that you will feel so helpless. You are not the first to be acquainted with sorrow, grief, or pain but the Master promises sunshine after rain.

In this book, you are required to speak into your life some powerful bible reflections selected for each chapter. Your sickness may be so threatening that you may have thought that it will end your life. You need to take up these actions and let the devil know that you are not giving up on your healing this time, and you will obtain it by all means.

Now, I may not know what exactly your sickness is; I may not know how threatening it is for you or all you've had to pass through. Below are some powerful action words of faith that you should begin to declare upon the sickness

• And He said, *"If you diligently heed the voice of the Lord your God and do what is right in His sight, give ear to His commandments and keep all His statutes, I will put none of the diseases on you which I have brought on the Egyptians. For I am the Lord who heals you." (Exodus 15:26 NKJV)*

Begin to pray for the divine grace to heed the voice of the Lord diligently. Ask for the strength to do what is right in His sight.

- *"If My people who are called by My name will humble themselves, and pray and seek My face, and turn from their wicked ways, then I will hear from heaven, and will forgive their sin and heal their land". (2 Chronicles 7: 1NKJV).*

Now is the time to seek God's face in all humility. Talk to your Maker, seek His face in prayers.

- *25. "So you shall serve the Lord your God, and He will bless your bread and your water. And I will take sickness away from the midst of you."*

26. "No one shall suffer miscarriage or be barren in your land; I will fulfill the number of your days." (Exodus 23:25-26 NKJV)

Are you willing to serve the Lord your God even in sickness, or will you allow that sickness to restrict you from serving God? Give Him the honor He is due. Pray to God for the strength to serve Him despite your health challenges.

- *"For I will restore health to you And heal you of your wounds,' says the Lord, 'Because they called you an outcast saying: "This is Zion; No one seeks her." (Jeremiah 30:17 NKJV)*

Pray that the Lord restores peace into your health. Pray that God changes your reproach from being bedridden. Pray to the Father.

- *"My flesh and my heart fail, But God is the strength of my heart and my portion forever. (Psalm 73: 26 NKJV)*

Pray that God should be the strength of your heart and your portion. Forever.

These are selected powerful action words from the scriptures. Pray alongside the scriptures. You should make use of these words to command your healing.

CHAPTER 6

GOD'S PROMISES CONCERNING LIFE-THREATENING ILLNESSES

"... I Am The Lord That Healeth Thee"

What has God said about this sickness? Have you paused to think of it? Or have you cared to ask from God His will for you in this sickness?

Of course, God's will for us is that we live in good health and have a fulfilled life. *"Dear friend, I pray that you may enjoy good health and that all may go well with you, even as your soul is getting along well". (3 John 2.)* But you still need to know what God is saying specifically about your situation as this would guide you on what next to do.

There are 1001 promises of God for the healing of various sicknesses in the bible. Still, when you ask God What He wants for you, He'll give you specific instructions and words to rely on that specifically relate to the nature of the sickness you are having, and that will guide you through your healing.

Has He not said in His words? *"If you listen carefully to the Lord your God and do what is right in his eyes, if you pay attention to his commands and keep all his decrees, I will not bring on you any of the diseases I brought on the Egyptians, for I am the Lord, who heals you. (Exodus 15:26).* This is more than just a promise of things to be done; this is a declarative statement of things He has done. It means "He is the Lord that has healed you".

Though there are times that it would look as if you are still having that pain, or still have to go through that surgery, or placed on life support and you feel discouraged... Yet in all these, He is the Lord that has healed you.

This is a powerful declaration that may seem hard to believe. It is a powerful declaration that requires strong faith to work. If you can't see yourself getting healed even when you are in pain, then your healing is still far away. I said earlier that there are more than enough promises of God for your recovery in His Word, but each of those promises need faith to be activated.

Believing in God's promises for your healing will not only hasten your recovery, but it will also give you supernatural strength and grace to pull through those moments of pain and agony that you won't feel the weight of the sickness.

The truth that you must know is, the sickness may not leave your body immediately. You may still have to stay some weeks in the hospital before you'd be discharged; you may still have to use those pills and have that surgery. But he will be with you through it all. You may lose the whole of your hair due to the effect of this cancer. But then, you have your hope assured in God that comes what may, you will get through this, and He will give you the strength to go through it all.

you're going to come out of all these agonizing moments with triumph, soon.

There are instances where God promised His children some certain things, but it took a long time before those people could get hold of the promises. Abraham is a perfect example here.

God had promised him a child, in fact, children, long before he finally got his first child. Would you then say God is a liar? No. It is because God doesn't work according to man's time. God works in seasons while man works in time. For us, the blessing or promise may seem long overdue, but for God, our thousand years are just like a day before Him.

This is why it will take you to have implicit trust in God and just believe whatever He has told you about your healing, then wait on Him to do as He has said. Because *"God is not human, that He should lie, not a human being, that He should change His mind. Does He speak and then not act? Does He promise and not fulfil?"(Numbers 23:19)*

David, after he has been anointed king over Israel, waited for ten years or even more before he finally was able to sit on the throne as king. The disciples of Jesus Christ waited for ten days in the upper room to get the Holy Spirit's infilling, which Jesus Christ had promised them even before He went back to heaven.

He has given you His words, that He has healed you. Do not fear death or any other effect of sickness that may happen, for when He sends His words, He makes sure that a jot of it does not go without been fulfilled.

Has He not said in Isaiah 55:8-9

"For My thoughts are not your thoughts, nor are your ways My ways," says the LORD.

"For as the heavens are higher than the earth, so are My ways higher than your ways, and My thoughts than your thoughts".

He will do just what He has said
for you. He is the Lord that has
healed you, and He will indeed
perfect His healing work in your
health. Yours is to believe Him.

Here are some of what God has said
concerning this sickness you are
going through

- *"For with God, nothing will be
impossible." (Luke 1:37 NKJV)*

This is an assurance from the word of
God. Appreciate the fact that no word
from God will ever fail. Adore Him,
for He is a God of all possibilities.

- *"Behold, I will bring it health and healing; I will heal them and reveal to them the abundance of peace and truth." (Jeremiah 33:6 NKJV)*

Pray for sound health and healing.

Pray this day that God's abundant peace and truth is revealed unto you.

- *"If My people who are called by My name will humble themselves, and pray and seek My face, and turn from their wicked ways, then I will hear from heaven, and will forgive their sin and heal their land.." (2 Chronicles 7:14 NKJV)*

Do not relent in prayers; pray and seek God's face.

- *"Fear not, for I am with you; Be not dismayed, for I am your God. I will strengthen you, Yes, I will help you, I will uphold you with My righteous right hand."(Isaiah 41:10 NKJV)*

Pray for the strength not to be overwhelmed by fear. Pray for the Spirit of sound mind and strength from above.

- *"...Thus says the Lord, the God of David your father: I have heard your prayer, I have seen your tears; surely I will heal you. On the third day you shall go up to the house of the Lord."(2Kings 20:5 NKJV)*

This is another excellent verse you should claim. Be assured that your prayers are answered, Yea! your healing is here.

- *"Now to Him who is able to do exceedingly abundantly above all that we ask or think, according to the power that works in us..."* *(Ephesian3:20 NKJV)*

Pray that the power of God would begin to work healing in your life from this moment.

- *So Jesus said to them, "Because of your unbelief; for assuredly, I say to you, if you have faith as a mustard seed, you will say to this mountain, 'Move from here to there,' and it will move; and nothing will be impossible for you. (Matthew 17:20 NKJV)*

Ask that God increases your faith.

Pray to God for the faith that can move the mountain of sickness, disturbing your health.

CHAPTER 7

BELIEVE AND RECEIVE

Matthew 7:7 is a great closure for your healing processes, not because it is a familiar verse but because it summarizes this devotional in the best terms. *"Ask, and it will be given to you; seek, and you will find; knock, and it will be opened to you. For everyone who asks receives, and he who seeks finds, and to him who knocks it will be opened.." [Matthew 7:7-8 NKJV].*

When a believer asks from God in prayer with faith, know there is the assurance of an answer from our heavenly Father. The Lord Jesus did a beautiful job by explaining to the disciples who were present to hear from him at the mount; those assurances are not just for the disciples of old but also the present-day disciples. In His sermon, He made it known through His teaching that not only does God knows what we need, He [God] equally wants us to ask until we have an answer to what we are asking Him.

HOW CAN WE APPLY FAITH IN OUR BELIEF?

Faith is the substance of things hoped for, the evidence of things not seen." Let it be established in our mind that we are praying to an unseen God, and if that be it, shall we trust in that invisible being to supply us with answers to whatever our desires or requests are. There must be an established opinion in His existence and His unrivaled power to grant our request even when there is no 'reasonable' evidence to attest that fact. This is what it means to believe.

Several examples were documented in the Holy Bible for our consumption and consultancy. The story of a leper who met Jesus along his way to a daily assignment is one that interests me a lot when it comes to the issue of healing. Upon seeing Jesus, he asked to be cleaned and in response, Jesus asked him if he believed that he (Jesus) could heal him; the sick man replied with a positive answer to express his undoubting belief in Christ. Interestingly, he was healed instantly. That is a great test of faith!

When we approach God, the first thing He looks out for is to see if we believe He can give us that desired healing. This fact is proven in Jesus's earthly ministry on several accounts; he was fond of asking virtually everyone who came to him, "do you believe I can do it?" This explains the irresistible importance of "believing" in the pursuit of "receiving" from God. *"And whatever things ye ask in*

prayer, believing, you will deceive"
[Matthew 21:22 KJV].

WHAT DOES IT MEAN TO RECEIVE?

While we pray to God, I can imagine how we are often eager for an immediate intervention from God over our situation, but that is not the only meaning to receiving. Jesus has stated the assurance that whatever we ask from the Father we would receive. *"Now this is the confidence that we have in Him, that if we ask anything according to His will, He hears us. And if we know that He hears us, whatever we ask, we know*

*that we have the petitions that we
have asked of Him." [1 John 5:14-15
NKJV].*

However, the word 'receive' has
been interpreted to mean different
things in human's vocabulary. I call
this a misconception! As much as
God would grant whatever we ask
from him, it should also be noted that
he won't grant our greed. James 4:3
as something to say in this regard:
*"You ask and do not receive, because
you ask amiss, that you may spend it
on your pleasures."* If your request is
not in line with His written purpose
for you, you probably may not get an
answer.

When you pray with faith, ensure you are not asking for your healing to the glory of yourself but God. You may ask yourself, "am I asking for healing because I want to be healed or because God wants me to be healed?" If you can provide the most appropriate answer to that question, it will help you apply your faith aright, and definitely, you will receive from God.

WHAT ROLE DOES THE WORD OF GOD PLAY IN BELIEVING?

Prayer is not just talking to God. A Bible scholar likened prayer to two-way communication with God. He added that it is holding an intimate personal conversation with Him. And, of the two, what God has to say is much more important than what we have to say. As written in the Holy Bible, the word of God does a lot to communicate God's opinion to us. It only takes effort to claim those words and promises according to what situation you might be going through.

The Word of God carries the inspiration of God, and it is quick and powerful; it can pierce deeply to as far as the bone marrow and even discern our thoughts and the intent of our heart. What a great thing to know!

At your ill state, when you receive God's message, hold tightly to it, giving no attention to any other voice that can initiate fear and unbelief to the heart. King David has been one of my mentors in this spiritual class; his faith in God is such a wonder.

"God has spoken once, twice I have heard this: that power belongs to God." [Psalms 62:11 NKJV]. Like David, when we realize that all power truly belongs to God and you strongly believe in Christ Jesus, you will no longer bother yourself if you will get healed because you are sure of i. God has told us that He is our healer [Exodus 15:26]. Again, King David testified to this truth when he wrote

his 103rd psalm, *"Who forgives all your iniquities; who heals all your diseases;"* [Psalm 103:3 NKJV]. Amazing!

Disconnecting from the word of God during the phase of sicknesses and illnesses exposes us to weariness. It can get so worse that it can breed unbelief and doubt about God's will for our lives. There is no cure for unbelief than the Word of God. Faith comes from hearing! Hearing the Word of God. You can grow your belief by involving yourself more in activities that expose you to God's word and His power: personal bible study, listening to Christian audio tapes, read gospel pieces of literature, to mention but a few. When you diligently involve yourself in these activities, you will be surprised how you grow in the grace of God. Let me close this discussion with another proven promise from the Holy Bible. *"But to you who fear My name, the sun of Righteousness shall arise with healing in His wings; And you shall go out and grow fat like stall-fed calves." [Malachi 4:2 NKJV].*

Do you want to take hold of this healing dimension of God's power? Then say this prayer.

PRAYER POINTS

- Thank God for reaching out to you in your unbelief.

- Pray for a sense of humor to push back against the threat of death.

- Pray for the grace to live in all positivity despite restrictions and fear.

- Pray for the functional things: The sunshine in the morning, the room with a window, for minimal side effects from medication, for divine provision, for every minute of rest and sleep, for the ability to eat.

- Ask that the Lord would increase your faith and help

you ask according to His
purpose for your life.

- Pray that He helps you to
glorify Him even in your ill state.

- Pray that He gives you the
strength to grow in divine grace and
knowledge.

- Thank Him because He has
answered and that you have
received your healing.

PRAYER FOR PERFECT HEALING

As the Bible has said, "The Lord is near to the brokenhearted and saves the crushed in spirit." And "He heals the brokenhearted and binds up their wounds".

• Lord Jesus, I have come before You this minute with a broken heart and with all humility. Forgive me for forgetting the weight of Your love for me. I come to You, and I present to You this illness threatening the life You have given me. You see where no one else can see, and You understand better than the Doctors. You understand my burdens and afflictions, and You know where I need to be set free. I know that You are redeeming and restoring; I ask for Your touch over this degenerating illness.

God of Heaven, I abide under the shadow of Your Almighty wings of love. I settle my life within your meek heart. I believe that my healing and restoration is in Your hands You are my Healer and my Redeemer. I confess my need to you today, visit me with Your grace and healing. Restore my hope in You and glorify Your name in my health. Forgive me for trying to handle my predicaments on my own; forgive me for spinning the wheel to seek help in different directions outside Faith and belief in You. Thou greatest Physician, I turn to You this time, relieve my pains and lift my burden. I place my worries and health in Your hands, Father, restore sound health unto me. Hold my heart close to Yours, give me the gift of eternal joy, restore health to my body, soul, and mind. Guide me towards my recovery, give me the discernment to recognize those You have positioned In my life for my healing.

I ask that You would stay close to my side and lead me through this tormenting phase. Help me to find calm inner thoughts within and peace in You.

I seek refreshment and healing. Be my Guide and the Author of my Faith.

Relieve my fears, show me Your mercies, by the assurance of Your presence, grant me peace within and an expectant heart. Help me to lean on You and abide fully in You.

Above all, Lord Jesus, give me the grace to admit Your will and understand that whatever You do is for the love You have for me. Amen.

CONCLUSION

There is no life-threatening sickness beyond the power of God. The Bible gives several assurances to the healing power from above. This book comprises of powerful prophetic promises and prayers that God has said concerning your healing. If you ask anything in His name, He will do it for you, and nothing shall be impossible for you if you believe.

Also, your faith is needed in your healing process. God may sometimes have other purposes for your trial; perhaps, the illness is to bring you into submission. However, for whatever purpose(s) God has for your trial, pray for a godly attitude through the pain, that God would use this crisis for His purpose and glory. Pray that the works of God may be displayed in your life this period, pray for the ability to endure with joy, and pray for wisdom.

Though, God may decide to take you through some healing process or give you an instant healing. Just know that whatever He does is to the glory of His name.

He is the Lord, your healer.

You are healed.

Made in the USA
Las Vegas, NV
05 January 2023

65085686R00063